A Product of My People

Keys Helland

Presentation by *BookLeaf Publishing*

Web: www.bookleafpub.com

E-mail: info@bookleafpub.com

ISBN: 9789357442077

First edition 2023

To my mother, my sister, and my best friend, who have never left my side throughout my dramatic relations with them and others.

To my deepest friendships and relationships, whether they be still in effect or in the past.

PREFACE

These poems I've written were not all born for this book, although some were. Most of my poetry sprang from moments of intense melancholy or euphoric creative inspiration. It was challenging to write for the purpose of publishing, but I'm thankful that each entry written for that purpose ended in a hopeful message. I've always said that we as individuals are just a product of our environment, but while accumulating this book I realized we are more so a product of the people who surround us. I wouldn't say I'm picky in the company I keep, but if we vibe, we vibe. I hope what I've written is relatable, enjoyable, and inspires you. Thank you for reading.

Pink Frosted Sugar Cookies

Sitting in a field of tiny pink flowers
Soft sunshine oozes up from the sunset
Friends sit around in a circle
Heaping plates of desserts in the center
Everyone smiling and enjoying each other

We're getting cookies tonight, you want some?
Do you want to make brownies tonight?
Why'd you make cake? Cause I wanted some.
Add two cookies to your order? Let's do it.
Let's go get ice cream together after.

Swooning, waltzing, frolicking in sweets
Vibing on the same wave, can't be beat.
My lovelies love sweets, my sweeties love me.
All such gracious reminders to enjoy little treats.

Sunflower Seed Kisses

Sunflower Seed Kisses
Like in old cartoons spitting out full auto
Coming with the scent of fried goods
I'd honestly rather you leave the habit than take
it
But I'm addicted to the affection like you are to
the confection
So I gladly accept your nutty perfection with
prospection
For as long as you're giving them with no
exception

My Best Friends Are Exes Now

When you told me
You were leaving reminders of yourself
So his heartbreak could linger and last
I didn't realize
It would crush my soul over and over
While he moved on
And I'm stuck on you're not here.

Now it's my cat that plays with your hair ties,
And it's my rolling table you wrote your name
on,
But it's our home you lived in,
We all partied in,
We cried in,
I came home to you in.

Now it's just me left in this empty home
Alone
With these tiny reminders
Of my best friend
And the fact that
It'll never be again.

Age of Eighteen

When I look at myself in the mirror,
I only see old and tired,
Like a father who's long past his prime with
three kids and a dead end career,
Or a mother whose children have left the nest
but will not give her grandkids.

I am not eighteen, I cannot be.
I've lived a thousand lives, I must be at least
eighty.

Some say when you die you're reincarnated as
another human,
until eventually you've been every human in
history,
and the people you are in the beginning have
young souls,
and the people near the end are old souls.

Why anyone is cursed with an old soul is a
mystery to me.
You're born old, and the longer you grow up the
older you feel.
When I was twelve, I was twenty.
I'm eighteen and I am eighty.

How old can a soul get before you shed your body?
Because at this rate my body will not be able to keep up with my soul.

The Variety of Relationships

Have a mother who takes care of you throughout the enraging but life saving bureaucracy you don't understand yet.

Befriend someone who sparks your drama queen dreams but goes to live them out in New York without you.

Find a friend in adolescence who will stay beside you throughout adulthood no matter the distance, distractions, or disagreements.

Date a girl who's the first to love you and go through traumatic times with her.

Date her husband simultaneously who provides the trauma.

Develop a friendship with someone who is endlessly kind to everyone but herself.

Date a party boy who calls you a fat cat in disgust and dances around dead people.

Befriend your best friend's girlfriend and stay incredibly close, until she gets another boyfriend.

Date a nice guy who slaps your ass every time you turn around and makes you inexplicably angry when you chit chat.

Befriend a young woman who shares your passion and worldview with better boundaries than you could ever have.
Date a guy who teaches you to love yourself but is ruthlessly cruel when he's hurt.
Date a girl who is the epitome of sunshine and still hugs you for warmth.
Date a man who offers you a safe space to grow and leaves you constantly wanting more.
Make friends with his and create a family outside of definitions.
Ultimately be born lucky with a sister who guides you, understands you, and supports you through all of life's fleeting moments and relationships.

Feel love in as many ways as you can.
Enjoy and learn lessons from everyone you meet.

...And I'm Left with None.

My bruise now faded
and consequently you too.
I'm sorry, but glad.

From you a sweet text
And a missed call from your mum
You both get closure...

Instant Message Support

When I'm somewhere with people
And I know I won't be heard
I couldn't get a word in edgewise with a crowbar
That's when I miss you the most
Because I know you'll let me speak until the tank
is empty
And you'll hear every word of it.

You tell me I will weather rougher nights
You tell me I will wander through tougher
storms
And your words will hold me
Til I die and from whence I am born

The Love System

This girl has taken a number from me.
Lovingly

10:25 I think of her.
She's a quarter, She's a dime
10/10, 4*25, she's 100.

I've never seen a number and seen a face
And seen her smile
And been blinded by her glow
I don't know, I can't see
Where this is heading to be
But I like where we are
And I like seeing stars
I hear the universe through you
Showing me the paths of mindfulness
Asking me to decide who I want to be
As I introduce you to me
I never thought things could be this easy.

Blazing Rebirth

You're so silly,
Singing love songs to the radio,
Giving yourself permission to enjoy everything
and everyone.
Your sunshine is rekindled,
Your joy is catching.
It's absolutely fatal.
The flame doesn't realize how limited its oxygen
is
Until the limitations are lifted,
And the flame bursts to life,
Starting a fire no one can put out,
Because you'll burn anyone that tries.

Magnetism of Opposites

He is hard.
He likes organizing, fast music, and efficiency.
He's stern and studious and surly.
And he likes me.

I am soft.
I like ballads, wandering, and magic.
I am sunshine and silliness and sensitive.
And I like him.

I make him hard, but he makes me harder.
He makes me soft, but I make him softer.
He's taught me to hold my boundaries with
others now that I can hold them with him.
I've taught him to honor vulnerability in himself
and strangers because he honors it in me.

We are built very different and that's why we
work so well together.
The grumpy one is sweet on the cheery one.
It's tropey, cliché, harmony, in love shit,
But I'm such a fucking sucker for it.

Temporary Goodbyes Feel Like Forever

Each morning on the way back to your place,
My heart aches with each passing mile.
My hand resting on your thigh since we left,
The grip gradually getting tighter,
As my ego throws a slow burning tantrum.
Squeezing at the halfway mark,
Clenching as we cross the first river,
A finger of the lake, and another,
Eventually turning into your neighborhood...

I don't want you to go.
I don't want to go to work without you.
Can't we just pause time and stay together?

Trying to hide my desperation for you
Keeping my cool & calm demeanor to reflect
yours
Matching your unwavering composure
You'll never know my inner turmoil
As we make our way out of the three day
weekend
And back to reality

Will I see you again?

Can you promise me it'll be soon?

After you get out of the car
Before you walk through your door
Kiss me like I'll never see you again
So I can cling to the feeling you give me
Because that's how I'll endure
Instead giving me the sweetest little peck
Leaving me selfishly wanting more.

Burnout

When I have time to myself nowadays I feel so
lonely
Maybe because now I'm just an empty shell
I can't even keep myself company like I used to
Even though I've always been my own favorite.

I miss you
I don't see you anymore
You're so distant
You're not taking care of yourself

My own fragility staring me down
Threatening me with work, lack of money, and
guilt

Shed your shackles
Shed your shackles
Shed your shackles

Everyone needs something from me
The expectations and demands overwhelming
My needs and wants are met with indifference
It's up to me and me only to take care of myself.

But I'm so tired I can't move
My pain so great I can't fix myself
The community so barren I can't get help

Help

16

Tragic Love Poems

Are you sick of me yet?
Are you looking for the exit?
You're asking me the same things
But I stay getting giddy from our good time
The bare necessities are feeling generous
After all this time getting fed scraps and specks
I'm on top of the world
Being valued higher than competitive markets
How have I tolerated anything else?
Why am I so craven for simplicity?
I want you to worship my existence
Drip fed and sucking at the spout
Weekly monsoons and I'm satiated for only a
day
Hangry for your presence
You're the ultimate stabilizer
Apart from you I endlessly spin into space
My tether, my bread crumb trail
A simple, gentle outstretched hand
Grounds me back home and into peace

This is vastly exaggerated and incredibly
dramatic
But while we're apart my heart bleeds tragic love
poems

It's all I can do to write and recite them
Until the next blissful encounter quiets my
emotions.

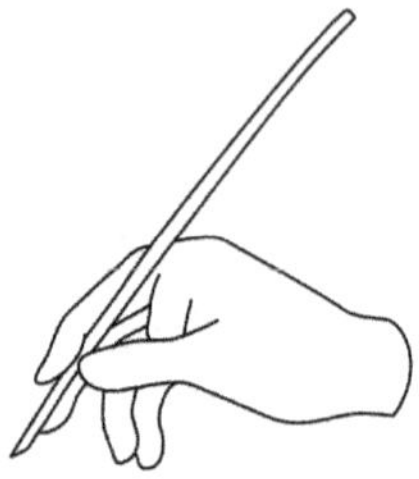

Realistically...

I'm not counting on you as a prescription
For this very haphazardly wired brain
But you remind me of my first toke
When my thoughts came in one at a time
This blissful peace is extraordinarily freeing
Like once again I have space to breathe
Space to think and dream
Space to very easily be.

And I'm sober now, haven't fiended for the weed
Because you naturally reduce the need.

These poems aren't to compare you to previous
partners, or my love to smoke
Nor to point out my glaring codependency...
Despite doing a good job at all of that.

The more I learn about you the more I celebrate
What an outstanding man I've met
Watch him charm those who witness his edgy
humor and commanding composure
His penchant nihilism and gentle vulnerability
His kindness towards animals and intolerance
for disrespect
The anti-door slammer and asker of opinions

The verbal promise and soulful cosmic vibe of
trustworthiness...

I cannot wait to learn more about you.
Everything I've gotten is a gift I adore.
The hardest part is waiting for more.
And I know we've got time,
It hasn't even been long,
But what can I say babe,
You make time together agonizingly appetizing.

The Move-In

On the way to your place
My heart starts to sink
Trained to tackle the trip of temporary absences
But here comes the hop up
This is not the bittersweet ride like before
Despite being the final trip
Because my home will now be one we share
And you'll be by my side
And there are no more goodbyes
Only see-you-in-a-bits

The Promise of Better

I woke up at 1:30 am today to go to the
bathroom
Snapped out of my sleepy state when my knees
didn't hurt to sit
Perplexed, could treatment have worked so fast,
is this a farce?
Got back to bed and felt the need to run
Not to run away, or run from my pain,
But to simply get my heart pumping again.
Overwhelmed by the new possibilities
I got giddy dreaming of all the things I could do
now.
A late night crying session is normal in my bed,
But tonight for once not caused by pain but
instead celebration.
I'd been given a second chance, and I promise
I'll do right by me.
This euphoria will not be temporary,
I can sustain this through due diligence and
discipline.
I deserve to feel good, I deserve to treat my body
right.
I love me so much.

I love you so much.
I will take care of you.
I won't waste this opportunity.
I will fight for our right to feel this good.
You are the most precious thing to me.
I'm so sorry we haven't felt this way before.
You have so much to live for and enjoy.
We can make it and I finally have the head start I
always needed.
I am abundance.
I am radiance.
I am ready and able to love you right.

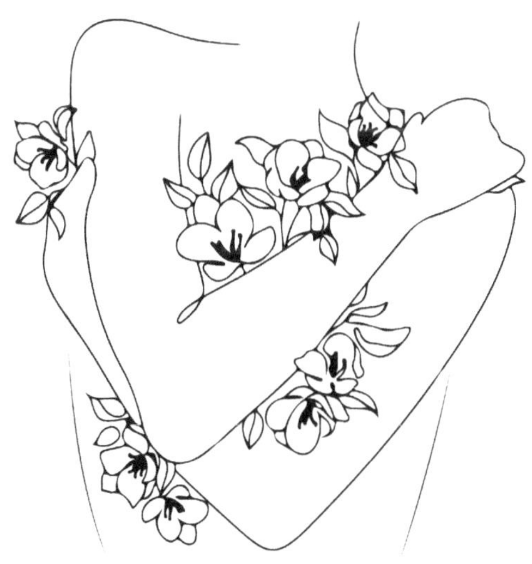

Two Days Later

A tidal wave of pain crashes over me
Too good to be true my hopes are slashed,
stomped, and burned
A temporary side effect of euphoria and health
Like a manic day but with the physicality to
back it up
I had applied for new jobs
I made plans to start new habits and hobbies
I actually felt like looking forward to something.
And now I can't barely walk.
Back to square one to start the measly climb
toward what felt so easy before
A taste of actual ability... such tantalizing
torture.
I'll take that determinism and apply it still
Just taking into account now, my lesser capacity
for gumption.
Week by week I gain one percent, two percent
functionality.
I was naïve to believe it could happen so fast,
But the possibility of hope still lingers,
The flame barely visible at the end of a tunnel
I'll crawl through mud and blood to fan the fire
As fast as this body will let me
But I've tasted victory in health
There's no way I'm giving up now.

Unapologies

Feeling unapologetic
Gonna be as loud and vibrant as I can
Without any mutism or downgrade
Making pretty just because I am

Don't come at me with your boundaries
You can silently slip away
I'm living life for me now
What's best for me, you always said

Existence is dazzling
Except for when it's not
In those moments I still find romance
Being sad can be kind of hot

Dancing down the street
In my flowy multi-patterned clothes
Blissfully loving you, me, and the world
Freely reciting empathic prose

New year, new me
Not necessarily always true
I'm embracing the genuity
Not inventing one to come into

Bold bright boisterous badges
Shouting love light and life
Disregarding the dusty decorum
Opting instead for overt optimist guise

Love me loudly
As I step into my reign
Love yourself fully
and I'll echo that refrain

Come with me and be unapologetic
Screw the world and their expectations
We are magic in our own definitions
They can seethe with their frustrations

Acceptance

Starting with my new name
Still sounds weird to hear it outside of my home
No fake pleasantries
A severe and freeing lack of censorship

Bringing in my crystals
Showing off my style (where I can)
Adapting my environment
Speaking up for my needs

Making jokes with the coworkers
Being vulnerable on the hard days
Naturally charming my vicinity
Being genuine is actually serving me

A mix of grumps and cherubs
A practical balance of moods
Fosters an environment of unity and assistance
One that I've personally never seen

"They're a close-knit group so don't worry if
you're not assimilated right away"
Doesn't seem like it's gonna be a problem...

"Don't be afraid to call out bullshit"
"Question everything"
"Speak up if you think something can be done better"

Joke amazon orders and lunch requests
Laughing at ridiculous movie trailers during our off-time
Poking fun at our unique quirks and personalities
Raging at outsiders and red-tape
Helping individuals and humanity contemporaneously
Forming, storming, norming, performing
Never looking forward to the adjourning

I'm Here

Is it the minimum or the maximum
The way someone loves you for your presence
alone
Sincerely happy because you're here
With the promise of you always will be

Such a soothing phrase
Sometimes the only thing we can offer
When there's a need for help beyond our means
Company can be the only securable comfort

I find my joy in people, they are your very
disdain
Yet I am your respite, relief, release
I am a person just like the masses
Not seeing the forest for the trees

One person cannot be your community
I tell myself as I tell you
What you love in you, what you love in me
We can love together in society

I'm here and I will be
For as long as I can
Let's continue to build our family
Our lives they can only enhance

The Year of White Lighters

I'm turning 27 this weekend
Finally discovering my desires and making plans
to act.
I'd always planned on keeping a white lighter on
me this year
Hoping to join the club of eternal youth
But as I'm rounding the corner, turning toward
thirty
I feel reinvigorated, youthful, and anticipative
Maybe I don't want to leave so soon...

I've always been old, at least since I was twelve
Now it feels as if I'm aging backwards
I've been told that youth is wasted on the young
Life is cyclical and your mind reverts near the
end
Maybe that means I am growing terminally
Well I guess we're all steady doing that

"I'm not eighteen, I'm eighty"
Kind of laughable now
Ten years later and I feel like I've just begun
All the new beginnings and opportunities on my
horizon

I'm entering this new era encouraged and enlightened
Clinging to the journey instead of rushing toward the end